PAPER CUTTING

PAPER CUTTING

CONTEMPORARY ARTISTS / TIMELESS CRAFT

Compiled by Laura Heyenga

Preface by Rob Ryan

Introduction by Natalie Avella

CHRONICLE BOOKS
SAN FRANCISCO

Library of Congress Cataloging-in-Publication Data
available.

ISBN: 978-0-8118-7452-6

Manufactured in China

Designed by River Jukes-Hudson and Matthew Boyd

10 9 8 7 6 5 4 3 2

Chronicle Books LLC
680 Second Street
San Francisco, CA 94107
www.chroniclebooks.com

CONTENTS

Were YOU the kind of CHILD that

ate your way all around the edge of the hole in the middle of a cookie bit by bit with tiny teeth in little nibbles?

Were you the kind of child who spent much more time drawing in the margins and making multi-colored borders and underlining the titles and sub-titles of your homework than ever actually doing it?

I was always busy jumping over and around the cracks in the sidewalk, and I looked up at the spaces in the sky that lay between the shapes made by crisscrossing telephone lines and power cables waiting for a jet plane or a bird to pass perfectly into the center of the frame that I had created in my head. At that instant, I shut my eyes as if they were a camera shutter and captured that moment and made it mine.

The world joins up with itself over and over again. Roads cross rivers on bridges; and one day you learn that rivers cross roads in aqueducts. Pavements turn sideways into pedestrian crossings, and then back into pavements. Tall buildings become one with the clouds, and airplanes draw lines in the sky with vapor trails that I used to look up at in wonder but now view with dread or even guilt.

I do like this whole paper-cutting thing.

I like the fact that I don't need paint or brushes or water or oil or palettes or canvas, just a piece of paper, a knife, and a pencil, and a rubber eraser. So much less—less mess, less waste, less stuff. More time—more time to say the things I have to say without detail getting in the way. No adding on of paint, layer after layer, and no more never quite knowing when to stop. Only taking away and taking away, first of all; all of the holes from the mid-dle of all of the doughnuts in the world, and then the tiny slivery gaps that exist in the spaces in some lovers' entwined fingers, or maybe that tiny little island of nothingness that lives between two pairs of kissing lips. And then a bigger hole that really is the entire sky, and so on and on until all the gaps fill up and slowly become the solidness that is the world we live in that somehow lies between.

Originally, I turned to paper cutting as a means to stop myself from putting writing into my work. I had always used small sentences here and there in my work. (I guess I just had things that I wanted to say.) However, these phrases had started to grow and extend to such an extent that my pictures were composed entirely of lettering. I had a small book of Tyrolean paper cuts of very pastoral images, rolling hills and gates and trees, wooden chalets, and cows with huge bells around their necks being led down from the mountains. These charming pictures had been cut through vertically folded paper and had perfect symmetry; I thought that if I worked that way, I wouldn't be able to put words in the pictures because they would be mirrored back to front on the facing side when unfolded. So I must admit that I was originally drawn to paper cutting by a form of self-censorship. However, I soon became transfixed by this world of perfect symmetry. It was a place where I could give the world my own imposed order, making it the neat and tidy place it so isn't.

So I started to make my own paper cuts from single folded sheets of thin paper with the sharpest scalpel blades.

In this new two-dimensional world, it was always good for people to be doing things, keeping themselves busy. This suited me because I like to be kept busy myself. People seemed to be constantly climbing up ladders or hanging upside down from the branches of trees.

I began to love living in the new world. It was a place where things always joined together and supported one another. In short, they helped each other out.

Clouds hung from tiny, finely cut chains as if they were a part of a stage set in a Victorian puppet theater. A forest of trees rose up to become a vast city of buildings, here a blade of grass, a daisy, a tree joined together in a solid shape to form a hill on which two lovers ran hand in hand against a skyline made up of shadows of trees that reached up to become part of a black sky as solid as a curtain out of which countless star shapes have been cut, through which the starlight of the heavens shines…

All connected, all one, all parts of each other on equal footing within the same plane. After all, we are all a part of each other, all interconnected and dependent on each other. When parts separate from the whole in nature, they wither and die, alone. These blackened shapes, their arms and hands reach out, always wanting to touch, their gestures are frozen in time as if the light had been thrown on and then hastily thrown off to their own startlement. But then, delicate as these flimsy pieces of paper are, they can still seem sometimes as solid as granite statues.

I think that the current artistic revival and interest in working with cut paper stems from a certain type of artist. One who loves to draw and also loves shape and solidity, but who does not want to be tied down by the weight of sculpting or the complexity of painting. An artist who wants to freely explore a material so light and fragile and easy to work with, with which she or he can create small worlds for us as light as our lives are themselves. The artist creates silhouettes in which we are mirrored, for after all in the larger scheme of things, our brief lives really leave so little behind after all the living has been cut out of them, that we are but shadows ourselves.

Rob Ryan

INTRODUCTION

Natalie Avella

In recent years, artists have been revealing just how expressive such a sparse material as paper can be when it is cut into. This paper-cut work merges many current creative trends: a simple cutting on plain letter-size paper can look minimal, and yet be highly decorative. Some of the most powerful cuttings are on white paper, with negative space carved or cut to create imagery. Rarely are more than one or two other colors added; the visual power of the cut is brought to the fore by white alone. There is no need for pen or paint, as the thin, dark-shadowed edge of a cut forms the decorative line.

Paper cutting puts us back in touch with the need to "make," to use our hands creatively and escape the pixelated imagery that is everywhere in our screen-dominated lives. Created using minimal material, a simple blade or pair of scissors, and no training at all, the paper cutting's sparseness and accessibility appeal in an age when banks are crashing, whole countries are going broke, and any signs of excess seem a little passé.

Yet, while paper cuttings can look very modern, paper cutting as an activity has a long, rich heritage. The Chinese, who first invented paper as we know it, started cutting more than a thousand years before most Europeans had even seen a piece of paper. The oldest extant paper cutting is a simple symmetrical circle from the sixth century that was found in a far western province of China.

There is no evidence that the ancient Egyptians—who invented the earliest form of paper by slicing, pressing, and pasting together the reed-like plant *papyrus*—ever decoratively cut this material. It wasn't until more than two millennia later, in 105 CE, that the Chinese invented paper similar to our own and the cutting began. The Chinese made paper by soaking plant fibers (such as hemp), beating them into a sludge, and straining the mixture through a cloth sieve attached to a frame, on which the resulting paper dried. The process was an amazing invention, and for many centuries other countries admired Chinese paper but were unable to replicate it.

Paper was at first a precious commodity, and as a result, paper cutting did not spread widely until after 600 CE. Cuttings, created with either scissors or a knife, began to be used to decorate doors and windows. By the thirteenth century, paper cutting was practiced in all parts of China. The most popular subjects were animals (birds, cats, monkeys, and so on), flowers (carnations, peonies, bamboo, and the like), and even agricultural produce such as beets and cabbages. Some cuttings were symbolic, such as the peach and pine for long life, the pomegranate for many children, and the melon for a rich harvest. Entire landscapes were sometimes cut, as were everyday life and work scenes of ploughing, feeding poultry, fishing, and weaving. Cuttings of leisure activities, such as children playing games and dancing, decorated the windows of village houses. In cities, cuttings of historical figures, folktales, and famous novels were popular. Chinese paper cuttings were almost always asymmetrical; although a symmetrical pair of cuttings was required for the two-paned arrangement of Chinese windows. The Chinese kept their method of making paper a secret, and it wasn't until 610 CE, as Buddhism spread east, that monks took their knowledge into Japan, where paper began to be made using fibers from the mulberry tree.

Elsa Mora *Hand* (detail), 2008, acid-free paper.

9

Once the secret of making paper spread to the Middle East (leaked, some scholars say, during military invasions of China when artisans bartered such secrets for mercy), the Muslims quickly built paper mills and developed machinery for bulk manufacturing. Baghdad became the world's first papermaking center, and mills were built there beginning about 794 CE.

In Turkey, paper cutting was recognized as an industry early on. Eleventh-century artisans were cutting pictures for the popular shadow theaters, and, by the sixteenth century, there was a guild of paper carvers. In 1582, the paper cutters are documented to have filed past the sultan exhibiting a beautiful garden and a castle decorated with flowers made of multicolored papers.

Paper was such a powerful commodity that the Christian church tried to boycott its use for many centuries, because it feared that the Muslim world was trying to dominate trade and culture through paper. The Jewish communities living and trading alongside the Muslims had, however, ready access to paper, and with this access developed a strong tradition of paper cutting. Jewish paper cuttings served religious or mystical purposes: there were cuttings to ward off the evil eye, to decorate the home on religious holidays, to indicate the direction of prayer, and to commemorate the deceased. Cuttings featured traditional symbols and inscriptions found in Jewish ceremonial objects and amulets, such as animals, birds, vegetation, urns, columns, stars of David, and the signs of the twelve tribes and of the zodiac.

The Christian church was forced to change its attitude toward paper when Gutenberg invented the printing press in the mid-fifteenth century and, until Europe became self-sufficient in paper production two decades later, the Ottoman Turks and Egyptians sold bulk supplies of paper to Europe. Paper was expensive at first, and the cutting of it was reserved primarily for religious purposes. In monasteries, hand-painted scrolls were sometimes decorated with cuttings.

Laura Cooperman, process shot, 2009.

Stencil making was a highly specialized area of paper cutting in Japan. Stencils were used to create decorative patterns on both the clothes of farmers and the elegant costumes of samurai. Artisans were masters of individual patterns, such as stripes or floral motifs, and used very precise tools and numerous cutting methods. The earliest stencil technique made use of a sharp semicircular blade producing hundreds of tiny holes. Stencils were created out of sheets of waterproofed mulberry-bark paper that was made strong yet mal-leable with persimmon juice or tannin. Treated paper was seasoned for three to fifteen years before it was used.

When paper cutting as an art form in and of itself really took off in Japan's *Edo* period (1615–1868), it became evident that the Japanese enjoyed seeing symmetry in their designs. Folk cutting called *mon kiri* involved folding a square sheet of paper, on which a drawing was cut to reveal a beautiful pattern when unfolded. The cuttings, called *mon*, portrayed flowers, plants, birds, and animals, and were often used as family crests.

Nonetheless, ordinary Europeans had started making images by cutting other mediums before paper was readily accessible. Polish shepherds, for example, had been using their sheep shears to cut patterns into bark and leather. When paper became available, they continued to use their shears rather than switch to the more delicate cutting tools used by the Germans and Dutch. The distinctive Polish paper cuts, called *wycinanki* (vee-chin-non-key), were at first used to decorate the whitewashed walls of cottages before Easter. Later they were used not only as decoration on both inside and outside walls, but also to adorn furniture, cupboards, cradles, shelves, and even coverlets. Mostly symmetrical, cuttings included popular symbols such as the spruce tree and the rooster, a common symbol of the Easter tradition. Designs were often single-color cut, but in prosperous regions, different colors were used, and paper was elaborately cut and layered to create multicolored pieces.

Paper cutting took off with gusto in Germany where it was known as *Scherenschnitte* (shear-n-shnit-a), which literally means "scissor cuts." It was commonly used to write love letters. Young men made these letters that incorporated hearts, flowers, and extremely sentimental inscriptions, and gave them as tokens of affection to their sweethearts. Delicate and lace-like, the letters were cut with sharp knives and were sometimes embellished with painted watercolors. The Dutch also did a lot of cutting, called *knippen*, that was often used to decorate legal and religious documents, and the Swiss made bookmarks called *marques*.

In the seventeenth and eighteenth centuries, making silhouettes became a very fashionable form of paper cutting. At first a pastime of the rich, silhouettes grew in popularity, and eventually professional cutters went from place to place, often making pictures of whole families. A silhouette was made by casting a shadow onto paper, tracing it, filling the shape with ink, and then cutting it out and pasting it on a lighter-colored background. As photography developed, making silhouettes became less popular.

The great writer Hans Christian Andersen was an avid maker of paper cuttings. By coincidence, Andersen's fairy tales have influenced many of the modern cutters featured in this book. Andersen's cuttings were mostly made with an enormous pair of scissors, by cutting into white paper that was then mounted on black. Some of his cuttings were simple figures created in a few seconds; while others were more elaborate pieces made by folding and cutting, then re-folding and re-cutting, creating ever more complicated symmetries. Andersen often cut in front of an audience as part of an evening's entertainment, accompanying the cutting with the telling of a tale.

Germanic people fleeing religious persecution in Europe brought paper cutting to the American colonies in the late seventeenth century, and Lancaster County in Pennsylvania became a center for the craft. Thus, paper cutting spread from China to Asia, Europe, and North America. Independently of these cultures, the sixth-century Maya of Central America are thought to have developed a paper from the bark of fig trees and cut patterns. The Otomi Indians of this region are still cutting less delicate designs, mostly for the tourist trade.

Elsa Mora, process shot, 2010.

Paper Cutting Today

While they once adorned the walls and windows of village homes and were seen only by neighbors and family, paper cuttings today are more likely to be seen online and by a global community. Contemporary cutters keenly show the world their creations by posting them on blogs and Web sites. Many cutters generously share techniques online. Cindy Ferguson, for example, regularly updates her blog with templates. One week, the image might be a boy riding a dinosaur; another, a young girl walking with a tiger on a leash. Ferguson has even endeavored to make very small, simple templates to enable children to try their hands at cutting. Her style is quirky yet consciously accessible.

Etsy, an online shop that allows crafters to sell their handmade products, is a good place to discover and buy paper-cut art. Many artists have benefited from the self-generated publicity of their Web sites. Kako Ueda, for example, admits that she has been invited to exhibit by gallery curators who have seen her cuttings online.

Styles in modern paper cutting are, as a consequence of the World Wide Web and of migration, less defined by the vernacular. Whereas in the past you could often look at a cutting and tell immediately whether it was of Chinese or Polish provenance, today this is less possible. Many of the cutters featured in this book no longer live, work, or exhibit on the continent, let alone in the country, where they were born. Béatrice Coron is a French artist living in New York, Elsa Mora is a Cuban now living in California, Hina Aoyama is a Japanese artist living in France, Su Blackwell is based in London but travels to the States to make paper-cut television advertisements for the likes of Napa wineries.

Cindy Ferguson *The Knuckledragger*, 2008.

Despite its growing popularity, paper cutting remains a slightly obscure practice. Perhaps this quirkiness is also relished by the cutters. Cutting is not a class that you'll find in the curriculums of most, if any, art schools. It is almost always self-taught and is often discovered by cutters after they have specialized in or experimented with other artistic mediums. Cutters come from all sorts of backgrounds, but most of the artists in this book at one time specialized in fine art or design: Patricia Zapata is also a graphic designer, Elsa Mora was an art teacher and worked in a gallery, and Zoe Bradley's background is in fashion design. Nikki McClure is one exception: she made a book of linocuts called *Wetlands* while she was studying natural history at university. The book is so good that it remains in print at the Washington State Department of Ecology. Her work explores the bold imagery of domestic work and labor first created by Chinese paper cutters: mothers care for children, people sweep, and hands clean dishes or cut up cabbages for pickling. McClure's work emphasizes the need to use our hands to make and create.

Most of the artists in this book discovered that cutting can create an effect that paint or pencils can in no way emulate. For example, Chris Natrop, an abstract installation artist, was making large-scale landscape drawings with charcoal, but was unable to achieve the hard edge he desired. He began trimming away various aspects of his drawings to achieve contrast. Cutting felt good, and he enjoyed making an absolute mark. When suspended from the ceiling, his cut drawings suddenly became three dimensional, casting shadows that shaped even the environment beyond them. He liked the fact that a complete environment had been made with minimal material, and soon he found himself drawing with his knife.

Installation artist Mia Pearlman uses India ink to outline loosely where her cut should go before she takes scissors to huge pieces of paper. Her initial drawing is free form, because she doesn't like to become attached to an image that will inevitably change during the installation process. Her work examines the ephemeral nature of reality; the elusiveness of cloudscapes, for instance, has been the subject of one body of her work.

Artists who work on a smaller scale and on a single piece of paper tend to make very detailed and precise drawings before beginning to cut. Hina Aoyama's cuttings, made using a tiny pair of scissors, are as fine and delicate as lace. Her drawings must be exact so that mistakes aren't easily made and so that the scissors never have to be removed, the pattern formed by one continuous cut. For Aoyama, cutting is a long process involving a great deal of patience. Flowers and animals often appear in her cuttings, as do replicated handwritten letters. One stylistic element Aoyama shares with the other contemporary cutters featured here is the absence of symmetry in her design.

Rob Ryan's cuttings also include hand-cut letters spelling out whimsical phrases about love and longing. He starts by making a pencil drawing on a sheet of 80 gsm book endpaper. He then scalpels out every tiny detail of the illustration and sprays the resulting image with color. For Ryan, everything must link together. Trees and foliage intertwine, or city terraces are connected house upon house. Ryan found his niche as a cutter more than a decade after studying fine art and printmaking. His revelation was that paper cutting is more accessible, easier for his audience to digest. His original paper cuttings are highly sought after by collectors, and he applies his paper-cut imagery to other products, such as tiles and textiles that he sells in his own shop, which is based in a fashionable London flower market.

Hina Aoyama *Baudelaire "Fleur du mal,"* 2007.

Mia Pearlman *Influx*, 2008, paper, India ink, tacks, and paper clips.

13

Whimsical, fairy-tale–like worlds are also present in the X-Acto–cut work of Elsa Mora. Mora's work often features little girls with pigtails wearing hooped dresses accompanied by cut vines and animals. These girls, who are reminiscent of the protagonist of *Alice in Wonderland*, embody an edgy mix of naive curiosity and innocence. Mora's imagery often explores the disturbing yet magical transition from girlhood to womanhood. In *The Departure*, a girl holds a small bird, while above her a larger bird takes flight, an image suggesting a girl turning into a woman. In *The Hand*, an upward-pointing hand grasps a miniature girl, symbolizing a woman in the process of taking control of her own life. Sometimes Mora refers directly to fairy tales: in *Little Red Riding Hood,* the wolf and the girl pass each other a flower in a cut-out apple shape. The viewer wonders whether Little Red Riding Hood is giving the wolf the flower or the other way around.

Artist Su Blackwell cuts fairy-tale worlds into and out of the pages of yellowing old books picked up in thrift shops. Her books lie open so that a type-covered paper landscape is exposed. She cuts into this landscape, and then folds the cut-up images to create three-dimensional sculptures that remain attached to the page by the fold. Usually, a woodland scene is created, and sometimes among the trees is a paper-cut woodcutter's cottage glowing with a real light set within.

Photographer Thomas Allen also takes old books and cuts new life into them. He cuts around the characters that brashly embellish the covers of '40s and '50s pulp fiction books. Sultry seductresses and dashing cowboys are half cut from the page, then folded out so they stand three-dimensionally. The book's spine props up the sculpture and is often included in the photograph so that the book title can inform the little diorama and amuse the viewer.

Artist Yuken Teruya also uses discarded paper products. He cuts beautiful trees into pizza boxes, cardboard toilet paper rolls, and paper bags from take-out joints such as McDonald's and Krispy Kreme. He seems to be taking this paper trash back to the forest in his critiques of the depletion of natural resources and the disappearance of cultural tradition and identity. In one body of work, trees are cut and folded into the inside of take-out bags that are then suspended so that light filters through the cut spaces to illuminate the tiny trees within. The trees are cut re-creations of those Teruya encounters and photographs in his daily life.

Elsa Mora *Rain Girl*, 2008, acid-free paper.

Banknotes are the form of paper that undergoes metamorphosis in the hands of artist Justine Smith. She folds and cuts bills into strangely incongruous pieces such as vases of flowers, hand grenades, and bouncing pet dogs. Her art examines money as a conduit of power and looks at the value systems that surround it. She describes her work as examining our relationship with money in a political, moral, and social sense, while also exploiting the physical beauty of the bills themselves.

Zoe Bradley's paper sculptures embellish and beautify, rather than criticize, the temples of modern consumerism. Her large cut-paper flowers and splendid paper gowns are displayed in the windows or on the floors of luxury fashion boutiques such as Louis Vuitton, Donna Karan, Tiffany & Co., and Missoni. Bradley works with paper as though it were fabric, and pleating is a signature feature of her work. Although she prefers the hand-created look, her commissions are often so large in scale that they have to be die-cut. Her large-scale work is hugely theatrical—the flowers and gowns look like they belong on the set of an opera—and it comes as no surprise that she once worked for fashion designer Alexander McQueen.

Matthew Sporzynski is another paper artist courted by the fashion industry; he has created sculptural works for the likes of Estée Lauder and Ralph Lauren. Sporzynski is especially known for his paper food—from a pint of strawberries to a pack of French fries to a mug of cappuccino with some cookies on the side. His sculptures are three-dimensional and life-size: the paper popcorn in the paper bowl looks inviting enough that you might help yourself. His paper sculptures are usually photographed for magazine editorials.

The colorful quilling practiced by Yulia Brodskaya is certainly an unusual style of illustration that has been photographed for many editorial and advertising projects recently. Quilling is a technique that involves strands of paper that are wrapped around a quill to form a coil shape. Brodskaya's colorful, curling pieces of paper are arranged on a flat sheet of paper so that one long edge of each strand sits up three-dimensionally off the page. For the cover of *Nico* magazine, she created a cover girl with long curling strands of paper hair draped around her shoulders. Brodskaya's quilling could be admired by millions on a recent Starbucks ad campaign for instant coffee; a swirling paper design was used to symbolize the company's desire to be seen as fresh, new, and oh so current.

Su Blackwell and Rob Ryan are frequently commissioned to create editorial pieces, especially for fashion magazines; their cuttings have been photographed for style magazines such as *Vogue* and *Elle*. Ryan has also collaborated directly with fashion designer Paul Smith. Italian installation artist Andrea Mastrovito was commissioned by Dior to create nine thousand black butterflies to swirl across the walls and ceiling of a boutique, making it resemble a contemporary art gallery rather than a fashion emporium. Bologna-based Mastrovito is known for large-scale tissue-paper collages held together with thousands of pins. One of his themes is transparency, and he literally reveals his creative processes or devices by using tissue, the most frail and translucent of papers.

Justine Smith *Specimen (II) Poppy*, 2005, Chinese yuan, wire, fly, and acrylic dome.

From large-scale gallery installations to small-scale shadow boxes, three-dimensionality is the quality that attracts many artists to paper cutting. Kako Ueda describes cut paper as a "two and a half" dimensional medium. Ueda's cuttings explore the ways organic beings are constantly being modified by culture. Her images are of insects, animals, and humans, delicately cut and often on red paper. She explores decay and the cycle of life and death; in *The Tree of Life*, for instance, a human morphs into a tree.

Helen Musselwhite's colorful woodland worlds are a more nostalgic view of nature. She uses several pieces of colored paper that are cut and layered onto each other, and then framed so that they are viewed within a box. Cutter Molly Jey works with similar themes, featuring woodland creatures such as owls, deer, and hedgehogs. Jey's work often uses layers of white upon white so that, for example, the branches of trees seem to intertwine. Emma van Leest is another artist who creates intricate shadowbox worlds. Her paper cuttings are boxed or framed so that there is large enough space between the cutting and the background to create a dramatic, shadow-filled atmosphere.

Casey Ruble is an artist who uses layering—layers of painted paper—in her images of Japanese warfare. Costumed, mounted warriors are set against natural elements. There is no blood, dirt, or gore, however, and the eye tends to be drawn to the decorative patterns on the costumes, patterns that are derived from such diverse influences as Islamic architecture, Art Nouveau, and Chinese latticework. Ruble says she cuts out the figures in order to deprive them of a cohesive, perspective-oriented space in which to exist.

Patricia Zapata makes use of the three-dimensional quality of paper to create beautiful but practical objects such as lampshades, gift boxes, stationery, and calendars. South African Heather Moore and Emily Hogarth may live on opposite sides of the Equator, but both have a similar interest in applying paper-cut design to textiles. Pattern and repetition are important in their designs. Moore's fabric includes "herds," which feature repeated patterns of a single cow from a cave painting or a repeated solitary mongoose, horse, or deer. Her fabric is sold by the meter and is readily made into cushions, tea towels, or aprons. Hogarth's imagery borrows primarily from nature, including highland cattle, mountains, and flowers. She focuses on the pattern and geometry that can be found in the natural world; a recurring interest seems to be flowers with big, bold petals.

While many paper-cut artists explore themes in nature—trees being a common paper-cut motif—Laura Cooperman explores the built environment. She grew up in a family of architects, surrounded by the houses her father and grandfather built. Her paper-cut buildings are extremely delicate, yet as detailed as CAD drawings—they seem to hang precariously from the walls on which they are exhibited. They explore light, depth, and movement. Her cuttings are engineering feats in miniature: despite looking tremendously fragile, they have moving parts and rotating gears.

Béatrice Coron explores both the built and natural environments with her knife. Her large-scale Tyvek worlds are epic fantasias, full of narrative activity. Her fantasy cityscapes are one example. The inhabitants of *Tree City* live on an enormous outspread oak. On and around its branches, people camp, fly kites, ride bicycles, and hike. There are theaters, a museum, and kitchens inside the trunk where cooks prepare delicious meals for hungry cyclists and hikers at the end of the day. In *Flowercity*, buildings are giant flowers that open at sunrise and close at sunset, where people float around in propeller-driven bubbles. Inhabitants of *Balloon City* float alongside each other in their residential hot-air balloons, coming down for brief periods to plant and harvest the land.

Helen Musselwhite *Camellia and Butterfly*, 2007.

Coron does not just create idealized, playful environments, she also seeks to challenge and disturb through her cuttings. *Danse Macabre* is a series of cuttings that explores our attitudes toward death and mortality. In one set of images, skeletons seem to dance while listening to their iPods, perhaps symbolizing the indifference many feel toward their dreadful fate.

Peter Callesen, a Danish artist who creates both life-size and A4-size works, also dares to challenge. Callesen's cut images emerge from the page like little sculptures, with the empty cut-out area itself a feature of the imagery. He believes that the sculpture's attachment to this negative space gives the image an element of tragedy; it is as though the figures are trying to escape but can't. Birds can't properly take flight, and skeletons can't walk away from their graves. A continual theme is "the dying swan," which he explains is a hybrid of Hans Christian Andersen's "The Ugly Duckling" and a human figure. Callesen's swan symbolizes attempts to achieve the impossible; the imagery suggests trying to be somebody else or somewhere else but instead being confronted with reality and failure.

The artists featured in this book embrace and create many different styles, using very simple tools and materials. They also explore many different themes. The following pages are proof of how versatile and expressive the simple medium of paper can be.

Peter Callesen *Snowballs II* (detail), 2005, acid-free A4, 80 gsm paper and glue.

1

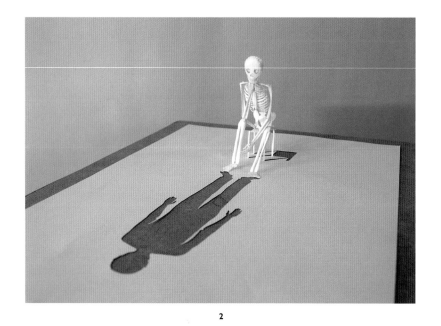

2

PETER CALLESEN

Peter Callesen has been recently working almost exclusively with white paper in different objects, paper cuttings, installations, and performances. The thin, white A4 paper he uses gives his paper sculptures a frailty that underlines the tragic and romantic theme of his works, many of which deal with dreams and the impossible. Another recurring theme is the reinterpretation of classic fairy tales associated with a more general interest in the lost land of childhood, between dream and reality. In the confrontation of these two conditions, a kind of utopian embodiment, the works become alive, often in a tragicomic way.

1 — *Impenetrable Castle II*, 2005, acid-free A4, 80 gsm paper and glue.

2 — *Looking Back*, 2006, acid-free A4, 115 gsm paper and glue.

3 — *Snowballs II*, 2005, acid-free A4, 80 gsm paper and glue.

4

4, 5 — *Fall*, 2008, acid-free 140 gsm paper and glue.

6 — *Closet*, 2005, acid-free A4, 80 gsm paper and glue.

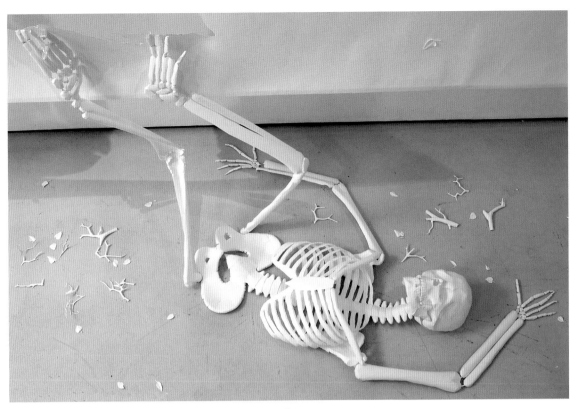

5

6

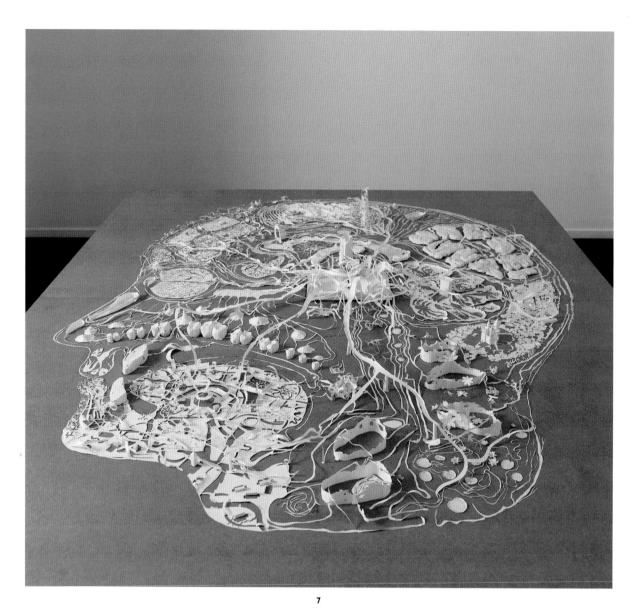

7

7, 8 — *White Diary*, 2008, A5 notebook, acid-free
120 gsm paper, graphite, and glue, mounted on MDF.

9 — *Distant Wish*, 2006, acid-free A4, 115 gsm
paper and glue.

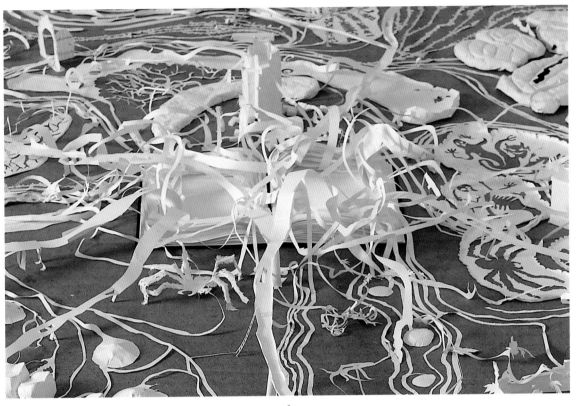

8

9

2

Having worked in pen and ink for years, **Heather Moore** enjoys the less predictable line made by her knife and the constant readjustments that cutting paper requires. She also likes the challenge of removing much of the surface and still having a piece of paper that hangs together strongly. Her process is simple and slow. She starts by drawing a composition on draft paper, and then tapes this to a sheet of black paper. Using a sharply pointed blade, she cuts through both layers, making adjustments along the way. Eventually, negative spaces are weeded out, rough edges are cleaned up, and the paper cutting is complete. Many of Moore's paper cuttings form the basis of her screen-printed fabric designs, which she sells under the label Skinny laMinx.

HEATHER MOORE

1 — *Waiting*, 2008, screen print, edition of 30, made after cut-paper work.

2 — In-studio shot of *Summer*, three *Protea* cutouts, and *Specimens*, 2008.

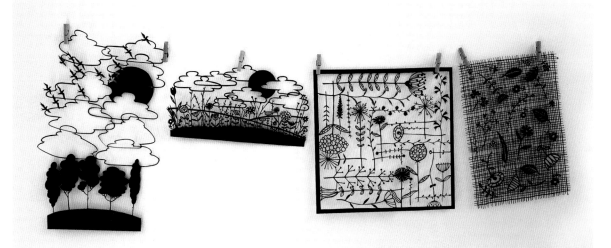

3

4

5

3 — *Escape*, *Flower Hill*, *Specimens*, *Flower Net*.

4 — *Flower Hill*, 2009, black construction paper.

5 — *Summer*, 2008, black construction paper.

6 — *Seeking*, 2008, screen print made after cut-paper work.

28

ZOE BRADLEY

2

3

Craftsmanship combined with dramatic silhouette is the hallmark of sculptural artist **Zoe Bradley**. Joining elements of sculpture, fashion, and theater, she creates elaborate, oversized silhouettes of highly crafted headpieces, dresses, and sets, often commissioned for advertising campaigns, editorials, catwalk shows, and window installations. Bradley employs traditional tailoring techniques, but offers a twist on the more conventional materials of fashion fabrics with her signature luxury papers. Her love of paper comes from a desire to find a material that can keep its form and is readily and abundantly available. She is always looking to push the limits of her material.

1 — Smythson, London, Nancy bag window, 2007.
2,3 — *Seeds of Peace*, 2007.

4

4 — Lane Crawford, Hong Kong, Christmas Highlight IFC, 2006.

5 — Platform 21, London, Folding, 2007.

6 — Liberty, London, Christmas Window, 2005.

6

8

I

2

Nikki McClure cuts each of her images from a single sheet of black paper. First, she draws with a pencil directly onto the paper, then uses an X-Acto knife to cut out the picture. The paper remains connected and becomes lace-like as the image emerges. McClure decides the width of the line and what will be black or white as she cuts. If she makes a mistake, she keeps cutting until a solution is found. Even though the work is careful and precise, there is freedom as she follows the whim of the blade. McClure examines our collective memory of hands working collaboratively: fixing, repairing, and mending as well as making, giving, and sharing.

1 — *Eat Out*, 2009, Strathmore charcoal paper.

2 — *Rely*, 2009, Strathmore charcoal paper.

3 — *Extend*, 2009, Strathmore charcoal paper.

3

4

4 — *Learn*, 2009, Strathmore charcoal paper.
5 — *Insure*, 2009, Strathmore charcoal paper.

5

6

6 — *Ebb*, 2007, Strathmore charcoal paper.

7 — *Resume*, 2008, Strathmore charcoal paper.

RESUME

8

8 — *Seal*, 2009, Strathmore charcoal paper.

9 — *Please*, 2009, Strathmore charcoal paper.

9

KAKO UEDA

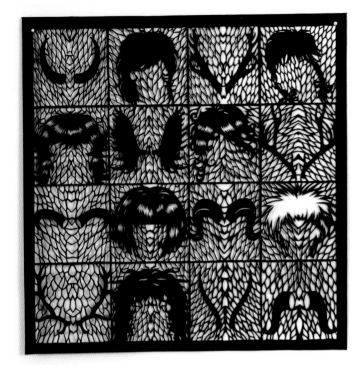

2

3

Kako Ueda is attracted to paper as a medium partly through her Japanese heritage, which encompasses traditional origami and the receiving of New Year's gifts of money in small paper envelopes. She often feels that she is in between two cultures—Japanese and American. It is an unsettling existence, yet it gives her insight into both places. The relationship between nature and culture is a recurring theme of her work: how culture alters and influences nature and vice versa. After all, the material itself is a product of nature (tree pulp) and culture (the invention of paper and its production), and the line between the two is constantly shifting and being blurred.

1 — *Contemplation*, 2008, paper and colored pencil.

2 — *Horns and Wigs*, 2005, black paper.

3 — *Allure*, 2004–5, black paper.

5

4, 5 — *Totem*, 2008, paper, collage, and string.

7

7 — *Oracle*, 2008.

8 — *PJS (portrait series I)*, 2006, paper and acrylic.

I

2

YULIA BRODSKAYA

Yulia Brodskaya was drawn to paper craft because she loves the material itself. For years she collected various kinds of paper, practiced origami, and made collages, paper sculptures, and handmade paper. More recently, with her signature quilling technique and intricately detailed designs, Brodskaya tries to show the potential for paper craft in general and quilling in particular to be used for a wide variety of creative tasks.

1 — *Tree with Birds and Animals (Darwin's tree)*, 2009, illustration for *New Scientist* magazine, January 2009.

2 — *Number 10*, 2009, illustration for *Libelle* magazine, May 2009.

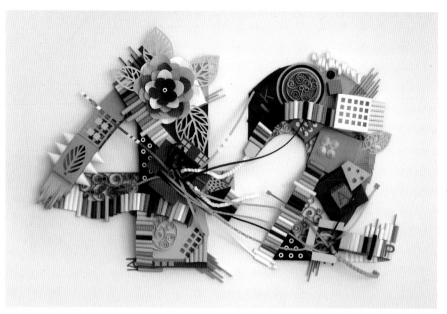

3

4

5

Su Blackwell began altering books in 2003 and has made a specialty of the art form. She is most widely known for her alterations of fairy tales and stories such as Lewis Carroll's classic *Alice in Wonderland*, and its familiar Mad Hatter's Tea Party. Blackwell cuts with a scalpel, bringing a scene to life by constructing three-dimensional figures and enchanting tableaus on the pages of text in which the narrative takes place. She often pursues the darker sides of the story, high-lighting characters who face eerie, sinister forests. A number of compositions have an urgency about them; Blackwell chooses characters who are about to discover something or who are perhaps escaping from something.

1 — *Magnolia Tree*, 2007, deconstructed book.

2 — *Alice: A Mad Tea Party*, 2007, deconstructed book in a box.

SU BLACKWELL

3

3 — *The Wild Swans*, 2008, deconstructed book in a box with light.

4 — *Wild Flowers*, 2007, deconstructed book in a box.

5

5 — *The Girl in the Wood*, 2008, deconstructed book in a box.

6 — *The Woodcutter's Hut*, 2008, deconstructed book in a box with light.

6

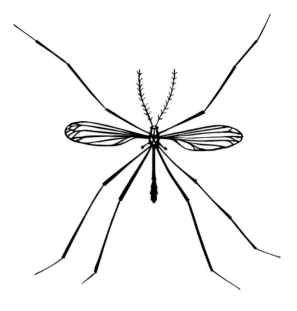

2

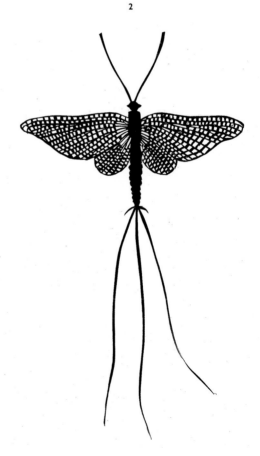

In May 2006, **Cindy Ferguson** went to visit her grandparents in the small German town of Hermuthausen. In their sitting room, they had a few traditional *Scherenschnitte* on the wall. The simple beauty and intricacy of the pieces inspired Ferguson to create her own. Through trial and error, she developed expertise in the technique. Ferguson gains much of her inspiration from silence. Freeing herself from the constant bombardment of everyday tasks helps her to be more creative and opens her mind. She also makes and distributes simple templates with the goal of teaching others and keeping the tradition alive and growing.

1 — Untitled, 2008. **2** — *Crane Fly*, 2007.

3 — *May Fly*, 2007.

3

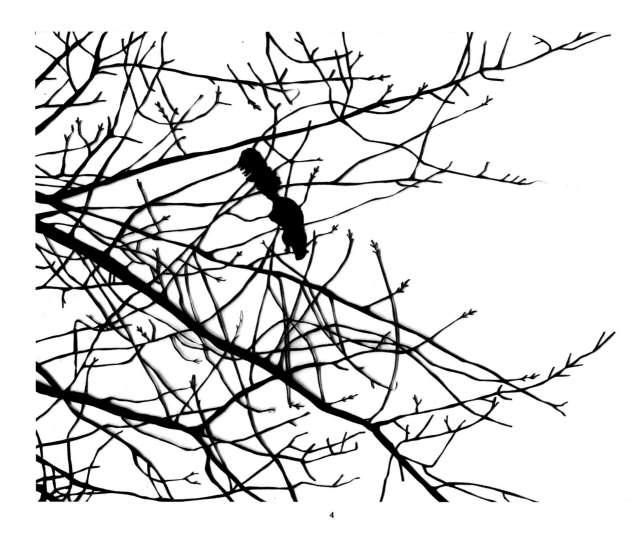

4

5

6

7

I

2

The creative process for **Helen Musselwhite** usually begins while she is walking her dog Earl along the lanes and footpaths near her home. The change in flora and fauna through the seasons is her muse. Color and pattern are important in the process too, and she often looks to nature for color schemes, not just in the wild but also in her garden. She also finds color inspiration in all forms of mid-century design, especially surface design and illustration. Musselwhite uses many layers to build up intricate and complex scenes through cutting, scoring, folding, and gluing. She is interested in telling a story and capturing a moment in time, a perfect tableau of a world that the viewer will want to jump into.

1 — *Summer Owls*, 2009. 2 — *Mini Pippin*, 2009.

3 — *Crowded Owl Tree 1*, 2009.

3

5

4——*Beauties Hedgerow*, 2009, paper cut in glass dome.

5——Detail of *Beauties Cottage*, 2009, paper cut in glass dome.

71

6

7

8

I

LAURA COOPERMAN

2

Laura Cooperman's intricately layered paper cutouts and architectural installations refer to a fluid space where personal, geographical, and physical borders fluctuate to challenge one's sense of place, origin, and home. She is captivated by the delicate, methodical process of paper cutting, and in her meticulous arrangements she experiments with light, depth, and movement. With movable parts and rotating gears, each work is an engineering feat in its own right.

1 — Installation from series titled *Breach*, 2006, paper and metal pins.

2 — Untitled, 2007, paper and metal pins.

3

4

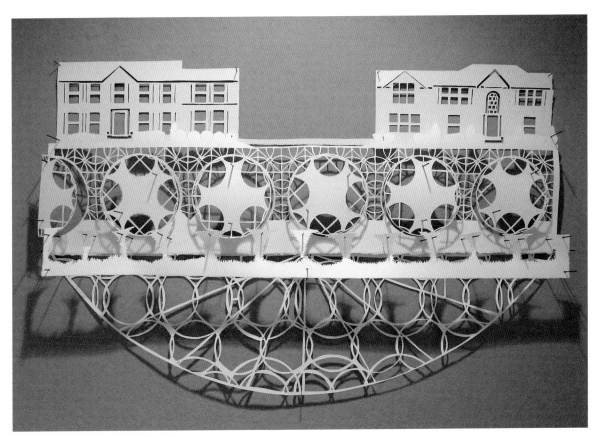

5

6

7

9

8—Untitled, 2007, paper, metal, and wood.

9—Untitled, 2006, paper and metal pins.

I

YUKEN TERUYA

2

3

Yuken Teruya manipulates everyday objects, transforming their meanings to reflect on contemporary society and culture. Cutting trees out of paper bags and cardboard toilet paper rolls, he creates meticulous and intricate artworks, small and enchanting worlds that relate to broader concerns. In each bag and roll, the shape of a tree is created without adding or removing anything, just by cutting out and folding the paper from the bag itself. Teruya's works explore issues such as the growing consumerism of contemporary society, depleting natural resources, and other problems associated with globalism, including the threat it poses to localized cultural traditions and identities.

1, 2— Installation view, *Corner Forest*, 2007, toilet paper rolls.

3 — *Pinocchio*, 2000, toilet paper roll.

4

4 — *Notice-Forest (Burger King)*, 2007, Burger King paper bag.
5 — *Notice-Forest (Japanese McDonald's)*, 2004, McDonald's paper bag.

5

2

3

ROB RYAN

For **Rob Ryan**, paper-cutting work means that everything is stripped down as much as possible. There is no tone, no variation of color, no pencil mark or brush stroke. There is only one piece of paper broken into by knives, and within this is the picture, the message, the story written and traced in silhouette. Ryan feels that this simplicity makes his work more readily accessible and easier to digest. His work is very much about sadness, being alone, and longing for love. People who have seen and felt his work tell him they find it reassuring and calming; this is why it is made, to help him settle and calm himself.

1 — *Nobody Remembers (Weeping Willow)*, 2006.
2 — *Other Planets*, 2009. **3** — *Clough Vase*, 2004.

4

THIS BELL WILL RING WHEN FROM NOTHING SOMETHING COMES

THIS BELL WILL RING WHEN WE DREAM A DREAM OF GOOD

5

6

7

7 — *Bell Park*, 2005. **8** — *My Home*, 2009.
9 — *My Heart*, 2009. **10** — *Big Book*, 2008.

8

JUSTINE SMITH

Paper has always been a primary material in the creative practice of **Justine Smith**. Her current work is concerned with the concept of money and how it touches almost every aspect of our lives. She is interested in currency as a conduit of power and also in the value systems with which we surround it. On a physical level, a banknote is just a piece of paper, but it is what a banknote actually represents that is central to Smith's work. Through her collages, prints, and sculptures, she examines our relationship with money in a political, moral, and social sense, while also exploiting the beauty of the notes' designs.

1, 2 — *Specimen (II) Poppy*, 2005, Chinese yuan, wire, fly, and acrylic dome.

3 — *Specimen (III) Kimilsungia*, 2005, North Korean won, wire, fly, and glass dome.

4 — *Specimen (I) Orchid* (detail), 2005, Iraqi dinars, wire, and acrylic case.

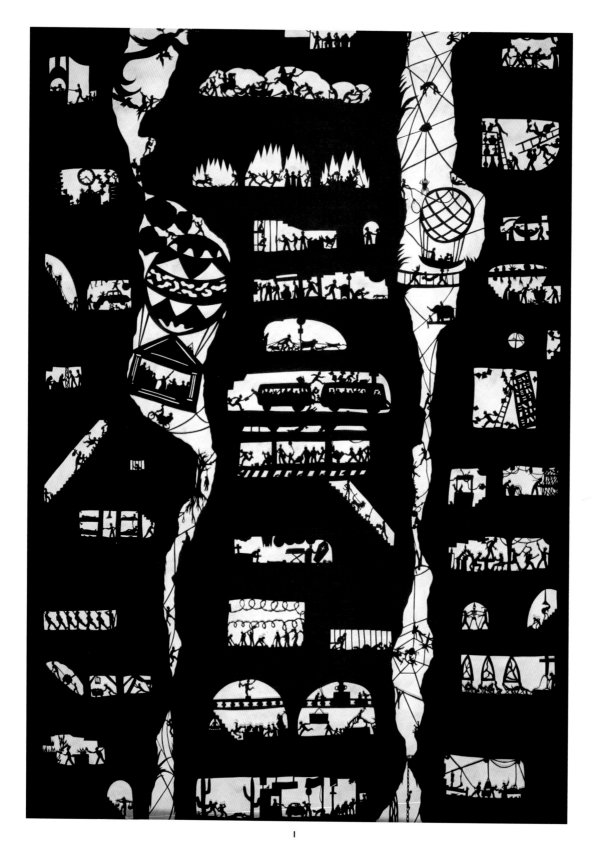

BÉATRICE CORON

Béatrice Coron's elaborately detailed paper cuttings tell stories in a personal silhouette language she has developed over the years. These compositions include memories, associations of words, observations, and thoughts that unfold in improbable juxtapositions. Her invented landscapes have their own logic and patterns. Fascinated by the situation of individuals in time and space and the memory process that filters their realities, Coron explores various narratives: one story leads to the next, and the creation process weaves together the layers of our relation to the larger world. The viewer is invited to find his or her own way into the creations.

1 — *Hells* (detail), from *Heavens & Hells*, 2009, Tyvek.

2 — *Penland or Road to Heavens Above*, 2008, Tyvek.

4

3 — *Heavens* (detail), from *Heavens & Hells*, 2009, Tyvek.

4 — *Hospitality*, 2008, paper.

5 — *Flowercity*, 2005, Tyvek.

5

2

MIA PEARLMAN

Mia Pearlman makes site-specific cut-paper installations, drawings in several spatial dimensions. Extremely sculptural and often glowing with natural or artificial light, these ephemeral weather systems appear frozen in an ambiguous moment, invading, escaping, or trapped in the room. Pearlman's process is intuitive, based on spontaneous decisions in the moment. She begins by making loose line drawings in India ink on large rolls of paper. She then cuts out selected areas between the lines to make a new drawing in positive and negative space. Between thirty and eighty of these cut-paper pieces are used to create an installation on site. Held together with paper clips and map tacks, these installations capture a weightless world in flux, tottering on the brink of being and not being. Pearlman considers her work and process a meditation on chance, control, and the transient nature of reality.

1, **2** — *Influx* (detail), 2008, paper, India ink, tacks, and paper clips.

3 — *Eddy*, 2008, paper, India ink, tacks, and paper clips.

3

5

4 — *Inrush*, 2009, paper, India ink, tacks, and paper clips.

5 — *Eye* (detail), 2008, paper, India ink, tacks, and paper clips.

6 — *Maelstrom* (with artist), 2008, steel, aluminum, paper, India ink, monofilament, and wire.

7, 8 — *Gyre*, 2008, paper, India ink, tacks, and paper clips.

6

I

MOLLY JEY

2

3

In her small cut-paper works, **Molly Jey** makes landscapes inspired by nature and imaginary worlds. She strives to bring the natural world into an everyday domestic setting. Her first works were all set in a white forest populated with creatures such as a lady wolf, a white fox, and a cardinal, which have become the mascots of her overall body of work. Recently, she made a series of three-dimensional floral works that mimic a scientific documentation of the natural world.

1 — *Daffodils*, 2008. **2** — *Camellias*, 2008.
3 — *Winter Chrysanthemum*, 2008.

4

4—— *Deer in the Forest of White Birch*, 2008.

5—— *Lady Wolf*, 2008.

5

2

Hina Aoyama works with a pair of scissors and the precision of a surgeon to transform paper into intricately detailed designs and delicate, almost lace-like patterns. Inspired by Matsuo Basho's haiku and the writings of Charles Baudelaire and Voltaire, Aoyama extracts passages and transforms them into meticulous works of art that appear to be laser cut. She is also inspired by nature, fantasy, and elements of her native Japanese culture. She mixes traditional and modern styles to produce a unique world of images, one that resonates with wonder, ethereal beauty, and magnificent detail.

1 — *La forêt harmonieuse les fées*, 2007.

2 — *Forêt de coeur*, 2008.

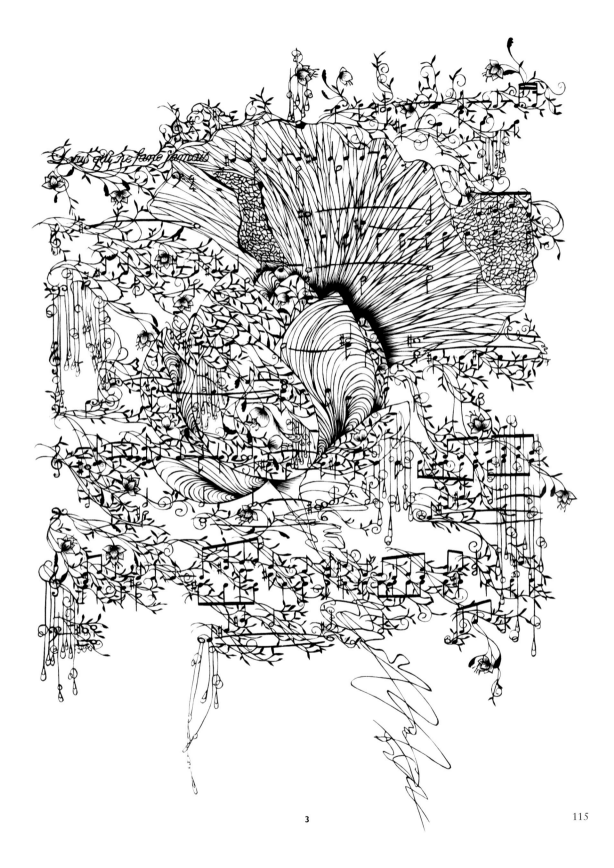

4

5

6

4 — *Lotus that Doesn't Die*, 2009.

5 — *Carrosse*, 2007.

6 — *Chandelier of Cherry Blossoms*, 2008.

7 — *Lotus that Doesn't Die* (details), 2009.

I

CASEY RUBLE

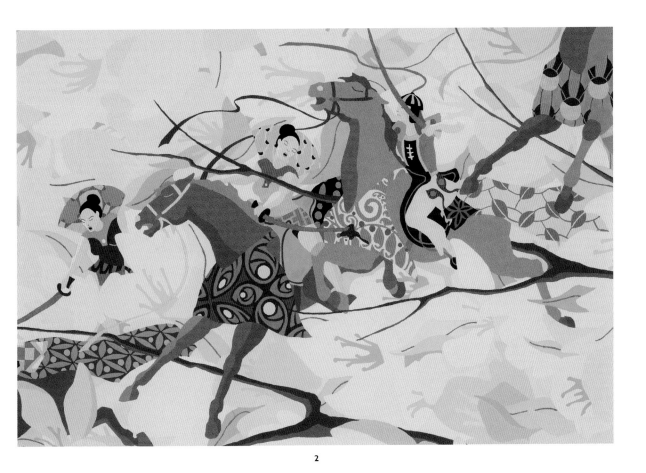

2

Paper and cutting are integral to **Casey Ruble's** battle-scene paintings. By literally cutting away the ground, Ruble emphasizes the relationships between the warring figures, eliminating the neutrality the ground would otherwise offer. The character of paper is a perfect fit with the battle theme. Both have a mind of their own—they warp and wrinkle, expand and contract. It's no surprise that people who work with paper use the word *breathe* to describe how the material reacts to its environment: paper does, indeed, seem very much alive, making it perfect for paintings that depict the fragile moment between life and death.

1, 2— *Isosceles*, 2008, gouache on paper.

3

4

3 — *Swarm*, 2008, gouache on paper.

4 — *Needle*, 2008, gouache on paper.

5 — *Zip*, 2008, gouache on paper.

2

CHRIS NATROP

Chris Natrop sees each piece of cut paper as a "knife drawing," created spontaneously without the use of patterns or preliminary sketches. Graphic silhouettes organically emerge from a meditative channeling activated by the repetitive practice of cutting paper. The work is often an amalgam of things he has previously observed, and the graphic nature reveals a particular sense of place. In many cases, one feature will be multiplied over and over, resulting in a dense layering of a single element. Emotional forces further contextualize the work within this structure: feelings of anticipation, apprehension, disorientation, or joyfulness often encapsulate the inherently myopic narrative. This fusion between internal, emotional space and the external, physical landscape is the framework for much of his practice.

1, 2, 3 — *Fern Space Burst*, 2004, hand-cut paper, colored ink, watercolor, iridescent medium, thread, pushpins, and cast shadows.

3

4

4, 5—*Far Beyond the Butterfly*, 2008, tape on cut paper
with painted stainless steel nail supports.

2

3

Matthew Sporzynski has always enjoyed making things from paper. These images are the result of a long assignment to create section opening pages (called *frontis*) for *Real Simple* magazine. Eva Spring (art director) develops the concepts and creates a thumbnail sketch that indicates composition and color palette. Matthew creates the objects from a wide array of paper (favorites include Stonehenge cotton watercolor paper, Canford cardstock, and seamless photo paper). He uses a range of techniques including papier-mâché, silhouette cutting, origami-style paper folding, and collage. Craig Thompson (set stylist) poses the objects for the camera. Monica Buck (photographer) captures the image.

1 — *Clothesline*, 2006.

2 — *Fireflies*, 2007.

3 — *Chocolate Cosmos*, 2005.

4 — *Wheat Sheaf*, 2005.

4

5

6

5 — *Leaning Tower of Pisa*, 2008. 6 — *Empire State Building*, 2008.

7 — *Big Ben*, 2008. 8 — *Eiffel Tower*, 2008.

7

8

131

9

10

I

2

Thomas Allen altered his first book at age five by tracing the outline of his hand onto the inside back cover of a *Better Homes and Gardens* storybook. Today, nearly forty-two years later, Allen's attention is directed toward releasing (with help from an X-Acto knife) and recasting the characters printed on the front covers of vintage pulp paperbacks, thus reviving and repurposing artifacts from a specific period in pop culture.

1—*Aroused*, 2009, cut and folded copies of *The Sure Thing* (1950) by Merle Miller and *Count Me In* (1953) by Fan Nichols.

2—*Outbreak*, 2009, cut and folded copies of *Asking for Trouble* (1956) by Joe Rayter and *I Get What I Want* (date unknown) by Larry Heller.

3—*Finale*, 2009, cut and folded copies of *About the Murder of the Circus Queen* (date unknown) by Anthony Abbot and *The Uncomplaining Corpses* (date unknown) by Brett Halliday.

3

4

5

6

4 — *Fever*, 2009, two vintage paperbacks (title/date/author unknown)—cut and folded.

5 — *Offshoot*, 2009, cut and folded copy of *Fugitive's Canyon* (date unknown) by Hal G. Evarts.

6 — *Pine (Remembering Andrew Sie)*, 2009, cut and folded copies of *Massacre Trail* (1955) by George Charles Appell and *Cast a Long Shadow* (1955) by Wayne D. Overholser.

7

7 — *Polecats*, 2009, cut and folded copy of
Nest of Summer Widows (1962) by Francis Loren
and three other unknown titles.

8 — *Epilogue*, 2009, cut and folded copy of *The
End Is Known* (1951) by Geoffrey Holiday Hall.

9 — *Cornered*, 2009, hand-cut copy of *Rawhide
Rider* (1957) by Thomas Thompson.

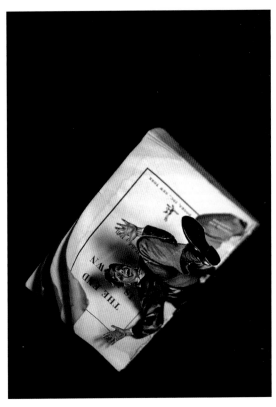

8

9

139

2

3

Emily Hogarth's relationship with paper started while she was studying textiles at Edinburgh College of Art. She found paper cutting was a quick way of creating sharp, bold, and uniquely individual stencils for screen printing. Today, she continues to be drawn to the delicacy paper brings to her work: the connectivity of the image and the shadows cast through the lines and the way they change as the daylight passes. Hogarth allows each piece to develop organically as she cuts. The elaborate patterns that emerge can be stand-alone pieces of art or can be translated into printed form, such as onto fabric or paper.

EMILY HOGARTH

1 — *Stag*, 2009.

2 — *Scottish Safari*, 2009.

3 — *Caledonian Wonder*, 2008.

141

4 — *Scottish Foliage*, 2007, black paper.

5 — *Stand Out in a Crowd*, 2009, paper and emulsion (screenprint of paper cutting).

5

7

6 — *Woodlands*, 2008, card and spray paint.

7 — *Midsummer Nights*, 2008, paper and emulsion
(screenprint of paper cutting).

8 — Untitled, 2007, black paper.

8

PATRICIA
ZAPATA

Patricia Zapata began her career as a graphic designer. In recent years, she has been dedicating more time to using paper for three-dimensional work. Her interest in the medium lies in creating minimalistic and nature-inspired designs that also have practical purposes, such as lamps, bowls, and wall art. Many of these projects and ideas have also flourished due to her interest in finding ways to reuse materials at hand. She also continues to expand her exploration of paper applications by developing tutorials so that others can apply her techniques and add their own artistic flair.

1—*Hold on*, 2007.

2—*Hiding*, 2007. 3—*Harvest*, 2008.

3

4

5

4, 5—*Exuberant*, 2008. **6**—*A watchful eye*, 2009.

PATRICIA B/07

I

2

EMMA VAN LEEST

Influenced by the feminine craft tradition handed down to her by her mother and grandmother, **Emma van Leest** most enjoys the alchemical process of transforming an everyday, common material such as paper into an object of value. She draws from sources as varied as Persian miniatures, medieval illustrations, botanical drawings and eighteenth-century lithographs, Indian comic books, and gardening magazines to create miniature worlds of myth and fantasy, harking back to the elaborate daydreaming of her childhood.

1 — *Simple Game*, 2009, archival paper.

2 — *No Repose*, 2008, archival paper.

3

4

3 — *Sanskriti Series II*, 2009, mixed media.

4 — *Sanskriti Series II*, 2009, mixed media.

5

6

5 — *The Dowsed Heart I*, 2008, paper, foam core, and glue.

6 — *The Dowsed Heart III*, 2008, paper, foam core, and glue.

7 — *The Dowsed Heart II*, 2008, paper, foam core, and glue.

ANDREA MASTROVITO

2

Andrea Mastrovito's layered cut-paper collages welcome us to walk in his world. The way he uses paper and pigment in the gallery space simultaneously references and defies a traditional concept of painting, first obscured by the simple gesture of cutting (as the knife replaces the brush), only to become evident again in the totality of the installations. Mastrovito's work comments on the internal dynamics of the art world and the spaces to which artworks are assigned.

1, 2, 3 — *French flowerbed*.

4 — *Italian flowerbed* (detail).

5

5—*John Holmes's Grave* (detail).

6—*English flowerbed* (detail).

6

ELSA MORA

2

For **Elsa Mora**, paper cutting is not only a form of expression but also a form of meditation. Through the process of creating paper pieces, she experiences a deep sense of connection with the material and with herself. She is fascinated by the endless possibilities of the medium, seeing a simple piece of paper turn into something meaningful. Each finished paper cutting is like a door opening for her. She is intrigued to see what it can be, and the feeling of exploration keeps her excited about her work.

1 — *Hand*, 2008, acid-free paper.

2 — *Bee*, 2008, acid-free paper.

3 — *Girl Carrying her Own Head*, 2008, acid-free paper.

3

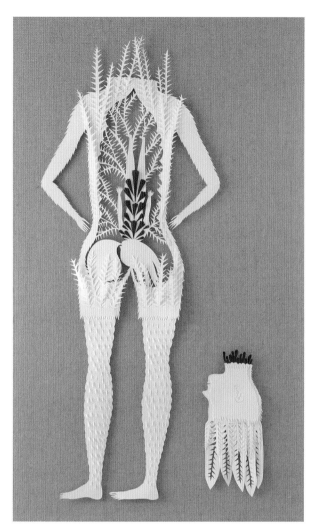

7

6

166

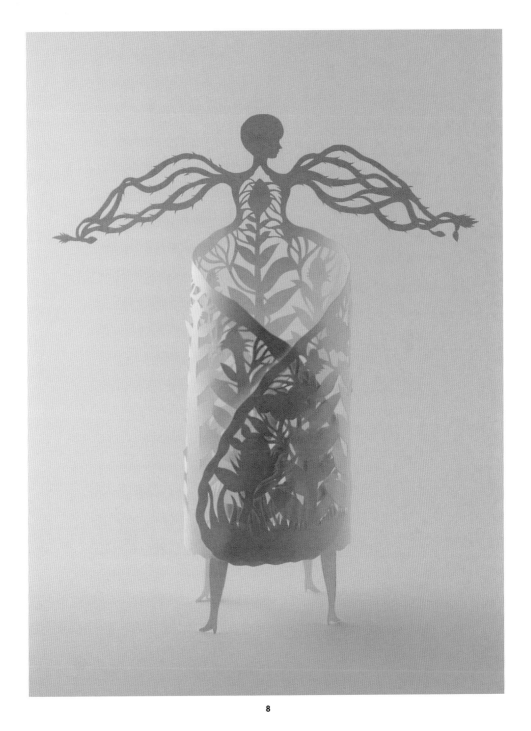

8

4 — *Broken Heart*, 2008, acid-free paper.

5 — *Girl Bird*, 2008, acid-free paper.

6, 7 — *Missing Thoughts*, 2009, acid-free paper.

8 — *Growing Woman*, 2008, acid-free paper.

167

10

9 — *Tree House*, 2008, acid-free paper.

10 — *Girl with Magic Fruit*, 2008, acid-free paper.

11 — *Bird Mask*, 2008, acid-free paper.

11

Thomas Allen (American, 1963) is an artist, freelance illustrator, and gentleman farmer. He lives with his wife, daughter, and a host of yardbirds on a 4.5-acre farm in Southwest Michigan. (www.thomasallenonline.com)

Born in Yokohama, Japan, **Hina Aoyama** (Japanese, 1970) has been making paper cuttings since 2000 and exhibits in France, Japan, and Switzerland. Her work has been included in numerous solo and group exhibitions, including a 2005 paper-cutting show at the Tokyo Metropolitan Art Museum; M.C.A./Salon international du Monde de la Culture et des Arts, Cannes-Azur, in 2006; Le salon des artistes contemporains at Honfleur, France, in 2007; and the Triennale international du papier at the Musée du Pays et Val de Charmey, Switzerland, in 2008. She has also received numerous awards, including the Gold Medal at the Le Grand Prix International M.C.A. Cannes-Azur, in 2007, and first prize at the Triennale international du papier in 2008. She currently lives and works in Ferney-Voltaire, France. (www.hinaaoyama.com)

Born in Sheffield, England, **Su Blackwell** (British, 1975) received her BA in arts and design from Bradford College of Arts and Design, followed by an MA in textiles at the Royal College of Art, London. She has had solo exhibitions in Australia and the United Kingdom, and has participated in group exhibitions in the United States as well as the United Kingdom. She has carried out commissions for many clients, including Harvey Nichols, and Beringer Vineyards, Publicis & Hal Riney, and Kate's Paperie. In 2010, Blackwell will hold a residency at the Bronte Parsonage Museum in Haworth, West Yorkshire, England. (www.sublackwell.co.uk)

Zoe Bradley (British, 1973) studied fashion design at Middlesex University. After graduating in 1997, Bradley went on to work with fashion designer Alexander McQueen. Her doily-punched showpieces for Spring/Summer 1999 were iconic and her experience at McQueen reaffirmed that her trademark would be spectacular silhouettes. Bradley went on to produce paper showpieces for Michiko Koshino and Liberty of London, which commissioned her to make a range of paper showpieces for their Christmas windows in 2005. (www.zoebradley.com)

Yulia Brodskaya (Russian, 1983) was born in Moscow. Before moving to the United Kingdom in 2004, she worked broadly in textile painting, origami, collage, and traditional fine art practices. Following an MA in Graphic Communication (University of Hertfordshire, 2006), she continued to experiment and explore ways of bringing together the things she likes most: typography, paper, and highly detailed, handmade craft objects. She has swiftly earned an international reputation for her innovative paper illustrations, and continues to create beautifully detailed paper designs for clients all around the world. (www.artyulia.com)

Peter Callesen (Danish, 1967) was born in Herning, Denmark. He first studied architecture, but then switched to art at the Jutland Art Academy and later at Goldsmiths College in the United Kingdom. Peter's career started with paintings, video, and performances, but he has more recently been working with cardboard and paper. He now mainly works with A4 paper. Many of his pieces take the form of three-dimensional figures created from silhouettes, and he focuses on playing with the contrast between the positive and the negative. Peter currently lives and works in Copenhagen. (www.petercallesen.com)

Laura Cooperman (American, 1984) was born in Cleveland, Ohio, into a family of architects and was raised a short walk from the buildings her father and grandfather helped to design. In 2004, she graduated with a BFA from the Maryland Institute College of Art in Baltimore. She has received scholarships and grants to study in Italy and China and has participated in a studio program in New York City. (www.lauracooperman.com)

Béatrice Coron (French, 1956) is a global nomad. Born in Chambéry and raised in Lyon, France, she has lived in Egypt, Mexico, and China. Coron launched her career as an artist in New York in 1984, and has since focused her work in paper cutting, book arts, and more recently, public art. Her work is in major collections such as the Metropolitan Museum of Art and the Walker Art Center, and her public art appears in subways, airports, and sports facilities, among other places. (www.beatricecoron.com)

Cindy Ferguson (American, 1975) was raised in Las Vegas. She won her first art competition in fifth grade with a drawing of a dancing, caroling moose for a Christmas card. Cindy graduated with a degree in design from Brigham Young University in 1999 and has worked as a graphic designer since then. Her favorite project so far has been to work in the Tower of London for a month creating eight large paper cuttings for their Children's Education Room. Currently, she lives and works in Salt Lake City with her dog, Starla. (www.cindyferguson.com)

Emily Hogarth (British, 1985) received her MA in Textiles from Edinburgh College of Art in 2008. During her time there, she developed and refined her interest in paper cutting. In 2007, she was awarded the Tigerprint Award at New Designers, London; the New York Tartan Week Award; and The Bonnet Maker & Dyers Textile Fashion Award, Edinburgh. Hogarth has since worked with Medici Cards, Studio Roam, Bebaroque, Tigerprint, Little Sparta, and Jasper Conran at Debenhams, among others. Currently, she lives and works in Edinburgh. (www.emilyhogarth.com)

Molly Jey (Swiss, 1978) was born in Locarno, Switzerland. Following a university degree in industrial design, she devoted herself to exploring ways to combine mediums and traditions to which she is most drawn, such as paper, origami, and craft art. Her work has been included in many European exhibitions. She lives and works in Italy. (www.flickr.com/mollyjey)

Andrea Mastrovito (Italian, 1978) received his MFA in 2001 from Accademia Carrara di Belle Arti in Bergamo. In 2007 he won the New York Prize, awarded by the Italian Ministry of Foreign Affairs. He has had solo shows in private galleries in Milan, Florence, Paris, Geneva, Brussels, and New York, and at the Galleria Comunale d'Arte Contempoaranea in Monfalcone, Italy, and the Centre d'art contemporain de Lacoux, in France. His work has also been included in many public exhibitions all across Europe and the United States—at MAXXI (National Museum of the 21st Century) and Palazzo delle Esposizioni, in Rome; B.P.S. 22, in Charleroi, Belgium; and the Museum of Arts and Design and the Italian Cultural Institute, both in New York. (www.andreamastrovito.com)

Nikki McClure (American, 1968) lives in Olympia, Washington. She is a self-taught artist who has been making paper cuttings since 1996. She has also written and illustrated several children's books and journals. Sometimes McClure collaborates with her husband, Jay T. Scott, making lamps, and with her son making gardens and large holes in dirt. In addition, she picks blueberries, swims in wild lakes, and makes tasty side dishes and an occasional pie. (www.nikkimcclure.com)

Heather Moore (South African, 1970) was born in Johannesburg. After studying English and drama at university, she moved to Cape Town, where she fell into illustration, and spent ten years teaching herself to draw. Moore uses her paper cuttings as the basis for screen-printed textile designs, which are now produced under her label Skinny laMinx. Her paper cuttings also find their way onto ceramics, wall decals, greeting cards, and screen-printed artworks. (www.skinnylaminx.info)

Elsa Mora (Cuban, 1971) is a multimedia artist raised on the island of Cuba, where she graduated from art school in 1991. Mora has shown her art in solo and group exhibitions in galleries and museums all over the world. Her work is currently represented by galleries in New York City, Los Angeles, Miami, Dallas, Portsmouth, and Bethesda in the United States, as well as San Juan, Puerto Rico, and Zurich, Switzerland. She has been a visiting artist at the Art Institute of Chicago, the Art Institute of Boston, San Francisco State University, and San Diego State University. In 2000, Mora won a prestigious UNESCO-Aschberg Grant. Mora currently lives in Los Angeles with her husband and their three children. (www.elsita.typepad.com)

Helen Musselwhite (British, 1967) studied graphic design and illustration and has worked in the creative world ever since, from an early interest in designing and making decorative home accessories to a more recent dalliance with jewelry design. Her love affair with paper began in 2006. Working with various paper types and nature as her muse, Musselwhite cuts, folds, scores, and layers to create intriguing and intricate views into a fairy-tale world of flora and fauna. She lives and works on the edge of south Manchester with one foot in suburbia and the other in the Cheshire countryside. (www.helenmusselwhite.com)

Chris Natrop (American, 1967) was born in Milwaukee, Wisconsin. He received a BFA from the School of the Art Institute of Chicago in 1992 with an emphasis in painting. Soon after graduation, he moved to San Francisco, where he began cutting paper in 2001. While in the Bay Area, he exhibited widely and was an affiliate artist at Headlands Center for the Arts. In 2004, he relocated to Los Angeles, and since then his work has appeared in solo shows at MOCA Jacksonville, Chapman University, and Sonoma County Museum, as well as in group exhibitions at the Armory Center for the Arts Pasadena, Holland Papier Bienniale, Winghall Museum, Vincent Price Art Museum, Taylor de Cordoba, Long Beach City College, and Florida State University Museum of Fine Arts. Natrop was the 2007 recipient of the Pulse Prize from the Pulse Art Fair, New York. (www.chrisnatrop.com)

Since receiving her BFA from Cornell University in 1996, **Mia Pearlman** (American, 1974) has exhibited internationally in numerous galleries, nonprofit spaces, and museums, including the Museum of Arts and Design in New York, the Montgomery Museum of Art in Alabama, the Centre for Recent Drawing in London, and Mixed Greens in New York. Her work is featured in several books on the use of paper in contemporary art. Pearlman has participated in many residency programs, including Proyecto' Ace in Buenos Aires, the Lower East Side Printshop in New York City, and the Vermont Studio Center. She is a recipient of a 2008 Pollock-Krasner Foundation Grant and a 2009 Established Artist Fellowship from UrbanGlass. Pearlman lives and works in Brooklyn, New York. (www.miapearlman.com)

Casey Ruble (American, 1973) has shown her work both nationally and internationally at galleries and museums including Nicole Klagsbrun and Black & White Gallery in New York; the Hunterdon Museum of Art in Clinton, New Jersey; Galleria San Salvatore in Modena, Italy; and Foley Gallery in New York, which also represents her. Ruble currently holds an artist-in-residence position at Fordham University, writes for *Art in America*, and works as a freelance curator. Her work and curatorial projects have been reviewed in publications including the *New York Times*, the *New Yorker*, the *Brooklyn Rail*, *Sculpture Magazine*, and the online publications *ARTslant* and *ArtCat*. (www.caseyruble.com)

Rob Ryan (British, 1962) was born in Akrotiri, Cyprus. He studied Fine Art at Trent Polytechnic and at the Royal College of Art, London, where he specialized in printmaking. Since 2002, he has been working principally within the paper-cutting medium. Although he views himself first and always as a fine artist, his intricate paper-cutting work adapts itself readily to screen printing on ceramics and fabrics and to laser cutting.

Ryan has collaborated with Paul Smith, Liberty of London, Fortnum and Mason, and *Vogue* among others. His work often consists of whimsical figures paired with sentimental, grave, honest, and occasionally humorous pieces of writing he readily admits are autobiographical. He lives and works in London, England. (www.misterrob.co.uk)

Justine Smith (British, 1971) was raised in Somerset and moved to London to study at the City and Guilds of London Art School from 1990 to 1993. She has exhibited in galleries and museums internationally and has work in the collections of the British Council, the United Kingdom Government Art Collection, financial institutions, and international corporations, and in numerous private collections. She lives and works in London. (www.justinesmith.net)

Matthew Sporzynski (American, 1967) was born in Ann Arbor, Michigan, and moved to New York City to attend Parsons School of Design. His exhibit in the Parsons Senior Show won him a freelance position with the International Division of Estée Lauder International, Inc., which sustained him until 1999 when he started his own company, Couturier de Cardboard Inc. Sporzynski has taught at Parsons since 1998. His work has appeared in *Real Simple, Harper's Bazaar, Town & Country, Vogue* (U.S. and Paris editions), and *GQ*. Couturier de Cardboard Inc. has produced work for the Estée Lauder Companies, the Museum of Modern Art, Polo Ralph Lauren, Tiffany & Co., Macy's, Saks Fifth Avenue, Christian Dior, and Hermès.

Yuken Teruya (Japanese, 1973) was born in Okinawa, Japan. In 2001, he received his MFA from the school of Visual Arts, New York, and in 2002, he received the Emerging Artist Award from the Aldrich Contemporary Art Museum in Connecticut. His work was included in Greater New York 2005 at P.S.1 Contemporary Art Center and was featured in the Yokohama International Triennial. Recent exhibitions include the Kunstwerein Wiesbaden in Germany; Free Fish at Asia Society in New York; the Shapes of Space at Guggenheim Museum; the 5th Asian-Pacific Triennial in Brisbane, Australia; and various gallery exhibitions in the United States, Europe, and Japan. (www.yukenteruyastudio.com)

Kako Ueda (Japanese, 1966) was born in Tokyo, Japan, and moved to the United States at the age of fifteen. She received her BFA from Tufts University, in conjunction with studying photography at the School of the Museum of Fine Arts, Boston. She earned her MFA from Pratt Institute, New York. She has exhibited her work in numerous venues including Smack Mellon Studios, Brooklyn, New York; DeCordova Museum, Lincoln, Massachusetts; Brooklyn Botanic Garden, New York; and the Contemporary Art Museum Kiasma in Helsinki, Finland. Her work was most recently included in the exhibition and publication *Slash: Paper Under the Knife*, at the Museum of Arts and Design, New York. She is represented by George Adams Gallery, New York. (www.kakoueda.com)

Emma van Leest (Australian, 1978) was born and raised in Melbourne, Australia, and graduated from RMIT University with a BA in painting. She stumbled upon the idea of paper cutting during a collage assignment. Over the years, she taught herself the medium and refined her technique, eventually finding it more satisfying than painting. Since then, she has exhibited all over Australia, and has traveled to China, Indonesia, and India on government grants. Most recently, she received a commission for the artwork for a Burton snowboard. She lives and works in Melbourne, Australia. (www.emmavanleest.com)

Patricia Zapata (American, 1970) received a BA in Graphic Communications from the University of Houston in 1994 and a BA in Biology from St. Mary's University in San Antonio in 1998. She has been an independent graphic designer since 2001 and owns Zapata Design (graphic design) and A Little Hut (paper goods). She has been featured in the HGTV program "That's Clever," and her work has been published in *Craft, CraftStylish*, and *Do It Yourself* magazines. She is the author of *Home, Paper, Scissors: Decorative Paper Accessories for the Home*. (www.patriciazapata.com)

Resources

A selected list of resources about paper and paper cutting:

Avella, Natalie. *Paper Engineering: 3D Techniques for a 2D Material* (Revised and Extended). Mies, Switzerland, and East Sussex, UK: RotoVision, 2009.

Cho, Minhee and Truman Cho. *Paper + Craft: 25 Charming Gifts, Accents, and Accessories to Make from Paper*. San Francisco: Chronicle Books, 2010.

Elliot, Marion. *Paper Sculpt Sensation*. Newton Abbot, Devon, UK: David & Charles, 2009.

Hagerty, Taylor. *Paper Cuts: 35 Inventive Projects*. Asheville, NC: Lark Books, 2010.

Hopf, Claudia. *Papercutting: Tips, Tools, and Techniques for Learning the Craft*. Mechanicsburg, PA: Stackpole Books, 2007.

Idees, Marie Claire. *Paper Crafts with Style: Over 50 Designs Made with Cut, Folded, Pasted, and Stitched Paper*. North Pomfret, VT: Trafalgar Square Books, 2009.

Klanten, R. *Papercraft: Design and Art With Paper*. Edited by R. Klanten, S. Ehmann, and B. Meyer. Berlin: Die Gestalten Verlag, 2009.

Leroux-Hugon, Helene, and Juliette Vicart. *Paper Cutouts*. Photography by Xavier Scheinkmann. Ontario, Canada: Firefly Books, 2007.

McFadden, David Revere. *Slash: Paper Under the Knife*. Milan: 5 Continents Editions, 2009.

Melischson, Henya. *The Art of Papercutting*. Minneapolis: Creative Publishing International, 2009.

Rich, Chris. *The Book of Paper Cutting: A Complete Guide to All the Techniques—With More Than 100 Project Ideas*. New York: Sterling, 1993.

Schmidt, Peter, and Nicola Stattmann. *Unfolded: Paper in Design, Art, Architecture and Industry*. Basel: Birkhäuser Architecture, 2009.

Smith, Raven. *Paper: Tear, Fold, Rip, Crease, Cut*. London: Black Dog Publishing, 2009.

Sowell, Sharyn. *Paper Cutting Techniques for Scrapbooks & Cards*. New York: Sterling/Chapelle, 2005.

———. *Silhouettes: Contemporary Paper Cutting Projects*. Asheville, NC: Lark Books, 2009.

Walton, Stewart, and Sally Walton. *Craft Workshop: Paper Cutting*. London: Southwater, 2005.

Williams, Nancy. *Paperwork*. London: Phaidon, 1995.

———. *More Paperwork*. London: Phaidon, 2006.

Zapata, Patricia. *Home, Paper, Scissors: Decorative Paper Accessories for the Home*. New York: Potter Craft, 2009.

Image Credits

13 top: Photo by Ikuo Hiramatsu.
13 bottom: Installation at Roebling Hall Gallery, New York. Photo by Jason Mandella.
16: Photo by Helen Musselwhite.
17: Photo by Anders Sune Berg.
18, Figure 1: Photo by Anders Sune Berg.
19: Photo by Anders Sune Berg.
20: Photo by Adam Reich.
21, Figure 5: Photo by Adam Reich.
21, Figure 6: Photo by Andy Keate.
22: Photo by Anders Sune Berg.
23, Figure 8: Photo by Anders Sune Berg.
26, Figure 3: Photo by Heather Moore.
26, Figure 4: Photo by Heather Moore.
27: Photo by Heather Moore.
30: Smythson, London, 2007. Photo by Karin Berndl.
31, Figure 2: Marithe & Francois Girbaud, Marithe Francois Girbaud New York, 2007. Photo by Marithe & Francois Girbaud.
31, Figure 3: Marithe & Francois Girbaud, Marithe Francois Girbaud New York, 2007. Photo by Marithe & Francois Girbaud.
32, Figure 4: Lane Crawford, Hong Kong, 2006. Photo by Joseph Cheng.
33: Liberty, London, 2005. Photo by ZB Studio.
34: Missoni Salone Del Mobile, Milan, 2008. Photo by Zoe Bradley.
35: Missoni Salone Del Mobile, Milan, 2008. Photo by Zoe Bradley.
36–39: Photos by Dan Kvitka.
42–43: Photos by Dan Kvitka.
44: © Kako Ueda.
45–47: © Kako Ueda. Private collection. Courtesy of George Adams Gallery. Photos by Adam Reich.
50–51: © Kako Ueda. Courtesy of George Adams Gallery. Photos by Adam Reich.
52: *New Scientist* magazine, Art Direction: Alison Lawn. Photo by Pixeleyes Photography.

53: *Libelle* magazine, Art Direction: Cilla Tibbe. Photo by Michael Leznik.
54, Figure 3: Photo by Michael Leznik.
54, Figure 4: *g2*, Art Direction: David Levene. Photo by David Levene.
55: Photo by Michael Leznik.
56–61: Courtesy of the artist and Long and Ryle Gallery. Photos by Andrew Meredith.
68–73: Photos by Helen Musselwhite.
98–101: Photos by Béatrice Coron.
102: Installation at Roebling Hall Gallery, New York. Photo by Jason Mandella.
103, Figure 2: Installation at Roebling Hall Gallery, New York. Photo by Jason Mandella.
103, Figure 3: Installation at Sears Peyton Gallery, New York. Photo by Jason Mandella.
104: Installation at the Museum of Arts and Design, New York. Photo by Jason Mandella.
105, Figure 5: Installation at the Centre for Recent Drawing, London. Photo by Mia Pearlman.
105, Figure 6: Installation at Smack Mellon, Brooklyn. Photo by Jason Mandella.
106–107: Installation at the Islip Art Museum, Islip, New York. Photos by Gene Bahng.
112–115: Photos by Christophe Jacquemet.
116, Figure 4: Photo by Christophe Jacquemet.
116, Figure 5: Photo by Ikuo Hiramatsu.
117: Photo by Christophe Jacquemet.
120–123: Courtesy Foley Gallery. Photos by Christopher Burke Studio.
124–125: Installation for the Headlands Center for the Arts, Sausalito.
126–127: Installation at MOCA, Jacksonville.
128–133: *Real Simple*, Art Direction: Eva Spring. Photos by Monica Buck.
134–139: Courtesy Foley Gallery.
150–155: Courtesy the artist and John Buckley Gallery.
156–161: Courtesy Foley Gallery.

DISCARD

Hina Aoyama *Chandelier of Cherry Blossoms*, 2008.